Evan
Skates

By Denise K. Cook

Illustrations by
Blueberry Illustrations

To Evan, with love,
and to all young new skaters.
From Nisee

My cousin invited me to his
birthday party at the roller rink.
He will be seven years old.
I'm six. I've never been roller
skating, but how hard can it be?
Besides, I like birthday cake, especially
when it's served with ice cream!

When I arrive at the rink on the day of the birthday party, my cousins are already roller skating. It looks like fun!

My grandmother (I call her Nisee) helps me get roller skates
in the correct size. I quickly put them on and stand up to skate.
I wobble and fall, skate a few steps, and wobble
and fall again … and again … and again.

The party was fun, especially the birthday cake!
The skating was OK, but not great.

But Nisee has an idea!
Nisee tells me that every time I visit her, she will take
me skating at the local roller rink. Great idea, right?

My next visit to the rink turns out to be much like the first. I wobble and fall, wobble and fall. So Nisee rents a skate mate to help me balance.

While I don't wobble and fall as much, I still need my skate mate. With it, I can skate slowly in the big circle with the other skaters. I seem to be getting faster!

On about the third visit to the roller rink, Nisee says, "Evan, I don't think you need your skate mate any longer."

"No, I still need it," I quickly reply.

"Then why are you twirling it around and around while you skate?" Nisee asks me.

"Because it's fun!" I laugh.

"I have an idea,"
says Nisee.
She always
has ideas.

"Leave the skate mate with me
and see how you skate without it."

"OK, I'll try. But if I can't ...."
I'll do this for Nisee.

I skate around the circle with only a couple of wobbles without falling and return to where Nisee sits.

"Nope, I don't need it anymore." I am surprised. Nisee isn't.

This is awesome. Every time I skate around the circle, I get faster and faster. Nisee is smiling.

I join the others in Hokey Pokey and all the other skating games. I make lots of friends.

While skating at the rink one day, the
manager announces something about races.

"Races will begin in ten minutes. Be sure
to listen for your age group." I'm listening.

I hear my age group being announced. I get to the starting line.
When the whistle blows, my quad skates bolt in front of the
other skaters. I'm winning, but out of the corner of my eye,
another skater races in front across the finish line.
Not bad for my first race.

Skating becomes a favorite when visiting Nisee. And I love racing and making new friends. Dad buys me some inline skates and I win most of the races at the local rink and at other rinks in the city area. Nisee and Dad continue to take me roller skating.

The ice rink at the largest mall in the city always has a humongous Christmas tree in the center of the rink during the holidays. I've never been ice skating, so I'm excited when Dad takes my brother, my sister, and me Christmas shopping AND ice skating. How will it feel to skate on ice? Will it be slippery? Will it hurt if I fall?

It's cold inside the ice rink. I'm glad I have a jacket. Dad rents the ice skates. When I put them on and stand up, they feel almost like inline skates. No problem, right?

Wrong! When I step onto the ice, it feels like a concrete slip 'n slide. My arms go up. My legs go out. I fall. And, yes, it's cold and hard. But I get up and try again ... and again ... and again.

I see the giant Christmas tree. It sparkles with hundreds of lights and decorations. I want to skate around it.

I stand up slowly and skate toward the tree. Now it feels more like skating with my inline skates. After skating several times around the Christmas tree, I feel like my skating self again. I skate better and faster.

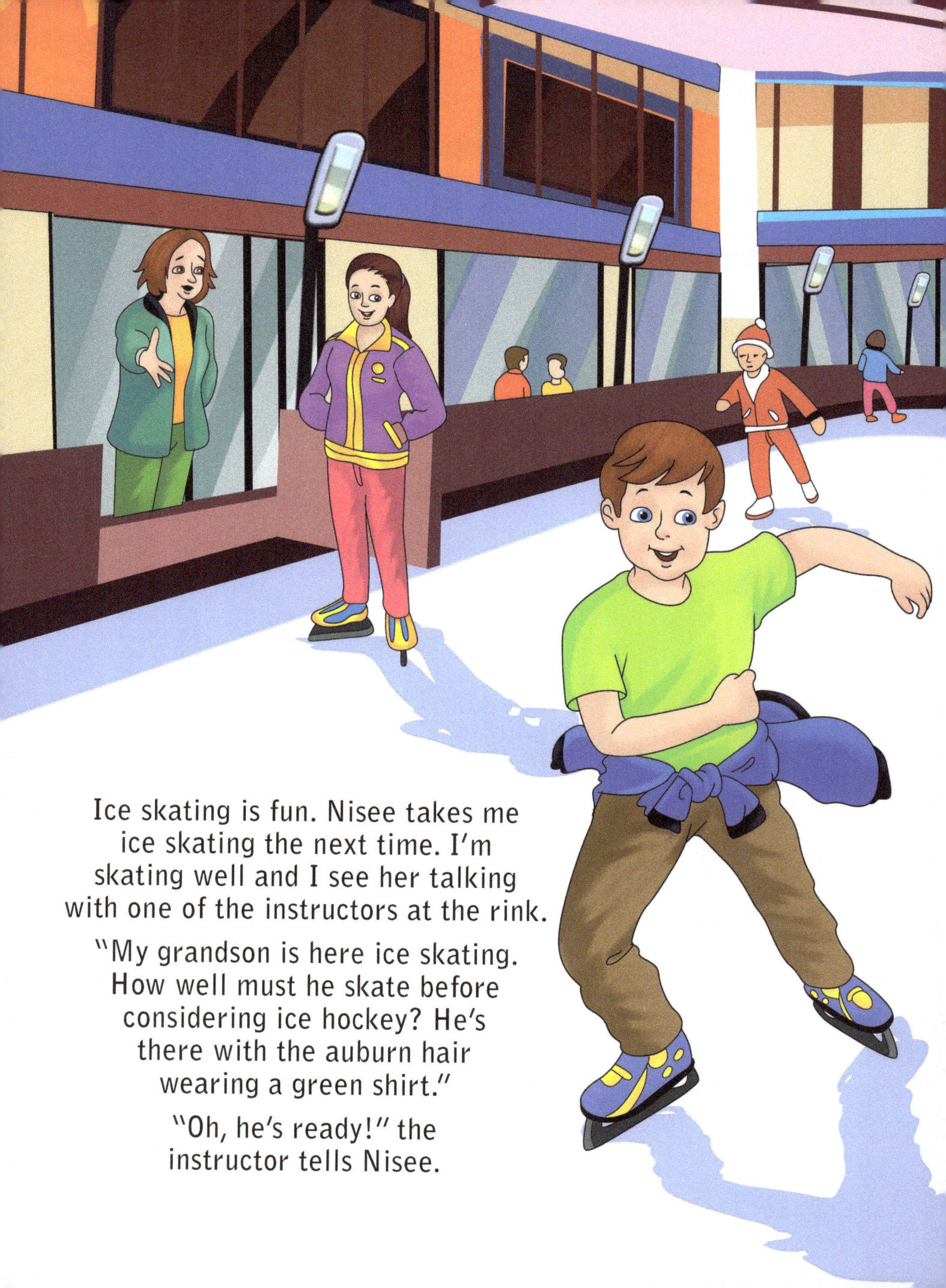

Ice skating is fun. Nisee takes me ice skating the next time. I'm skating well and I see her talking with one of the instructors at the rink.

"My grandson is here ice skating. How well must he skate before considering ice hockey? He's there with the auburn hair wearing a green shirt."

"Oh, he's ready!" the instructor tells Nisee.

It just so happens that Mom has a friend whose son plays ice hockey. Dad asks me if I would like to play ice hockey.

"Sure!" I say.

I'm eight years old now and I've learned a lot. In less than two years, I go from roller skating with a skate mate to

ice skating with an ice hockey stick!

Falling down may hurt.

But getting back up is exciting!

Denise K. Cook packed a suitcase full of costumes instead of the usual curriculum when she taught ESL to children overseas. As a grandmother now, she still enjoys the energy, desire, and imagination that children employ to learn new things. Today, she uses her degrees in language and education to write for children and to correct her grandchildren's grammar. Denise and her husband sponsor children through a program that helps release children around the world from poverty so that they, too, can grow, learn, imagine, and experience new wonders.